World-Changing SCIENTISTS

Rachel   Carson

Alix Wood

PowerKiDS
press™

New York

Published in 2019 by Rosen Publishing
29 East 21st Street, New York, NY 10010

Cataloging-in-Publication Data

Names: Wood, Alix.
Title: Rachel Carson / Alix Wood.
Description: New York : PowerKids Press, 2019. | Series: World-changing
scientists | Includes glossary and index.
Identifiers: LCCN ISBN 9781538337868 (pbk.) | ISBN 9781538337851
(library bound) | ISBN 9781538337875 (6 pack)
Subjects: LCSH: Carson, Rachel, 1907-1964--Juvenile literature.
| Biologists--United States--Biography--Juvenile literature. |
Environmentalists--United States--Biography--Juvenile literature. | Science
writers--United States--Biography--Juvenile literature.
Classification: LCC QH31.C33 W64 2019 | DDC 570.92 B--dc23

Adaptations to North American edition © 2019
by Rosen Publishing

Produced for Rosen Publishing by Alix Wood Books
Designed by Alix Wood
Editor: Eloise Macgregor

Photo credits:
Cover, 1, 4 top, 15 © US Fish and Wildlife Service; 4 bottom left and right, 5,
9, 10, 11 bottom,12, 13, 16, 18, 19, 22, 24 © Adobe Stock Images: 6 top
© Lee Paxton; 6 bottom, 8 © Internet Archive Book Images; 11 top ©
The University Press of Kentucky; 14 © Alex Kerney; 17 © R. B. Pope/USDA
Forest Service; 21 © White House Press Office; 23 © National Archives and Records
Administration; 25 bottom © Laura A. Macaluso; 26 top © Brocken Inaglory; 26
bottom, 27 © Alix Wood; all other images are in the public domain

Printed in the United States of America

CPSIA compliance information: Batch #CS18PK: For further information contact Rosen
Publishing, New York, New York at 1-800-542-2595.

Contents

World-Changing Scientist
Rachel Carson

Rachel Carson was an American **marine biologist** and author. She loved the oceans and nature. Her work and writing helped alert people to the danger of using chemicals in our environment. Carson's most famous book, *Silent Spring*, helped to start a worldwide **environmental** movement.

Science Notes

Marine biologists study sea creatures. They might study enormous whales, or tiny, microscopic life, such as algae. Rachel Carson was fascinated by everything about the oceans. She wrote about the creatures that lived in them, and the environment in which they lived. Her books were very interesting for anyone who loved nature.

When Rachel Carson was young, she had two passions. She loved nature and she loved reading. All through her life she never lost her sense of wonder at the beauty of the natural world. She made it her life's work to protect natural **habitats** from harmful chemicals and human greed.

"In every outthrust headland, in every curving beach, in every grain of sand there is the story of the earth."

RACHEL CARSON

Rachel Louise Carson was born on May 27, 1907, near Springdale, Pennsylvania. She was the youngest of three children. Her sister, Marian, and brother, Robert, were quite a bit older than Rachel. Their father was an insurance salesman, and the family lived on a 65-acre (26 ha) farm. It was wonderful to grow up surrounded by so much nature. Although the farm was large, the family did not have much money. Their home had no indoor plumbing or electricity!

Rachel Carson's childhood home in Springdale, Pennsylvania.

Rachel was a quiet child who loved to read. She liked stories about animals, such as Kenneth Graeme's *Wind in the Willows*. Rachel also liked to write. When she was 11 years old, she had one of her stories published in her favorite children's magazine, *St. Nicholas*. The magazine went on to publish several more of her stories.

APRIL 1916

6

Rachel's mother had been a schoolteacher before she was married. She loved nature, and she and her daughter would spend hours outdoors around the farm. Rachel's mother taught her all about the flowers and animals that they found at the homestead. Her mother also encouraged her love of books and of writing.

Rachel later wrote: "If a child is to keep alive his inborn sense of wonder, he needs the companionship of at least one adult who can share it, rediscovering with him the joy, excitement, and mystery of the world we live in."

RACHEL CARSON

Science Notes

Rachel's home in Springdale was near the Allegheny River, which also flows through the industrial center of Pittsburgh. Industry was booming in Pittsburgh. From Rachel's bedroom window, she could see the smoke from the American Glue Factory less than a mile (1.6 km) away. The smell was so bad people couldn't sit on their porches in the evening. Perhaps seeing this **pollution** sparked her interest in the environment at a young age.

At elementary school, Carson was a good student. She always got very good grades for her work. Her mother wanted to make sure Rachel got a good education. At age 16, Carson started at Parnassus High School, two miles (3.2 km) from Springdale. The teaching standard at the school was very high. She graduated first in her class.

Carson went on to study English at the Pennsylvania College for Women (today known as Chatham University) in Pittsburgh. She enjoyed writing for the student newspaper, but her love of science meant she eventually changed subjects to study **biology**.

A drawing of Pennsylvania College for Women from 1892.

Even though Carson won a **scholarship** that paid part of her college fees, her parents struggled to afford the rest of the money she needed to pay for the teaching and cover her living expenses. They sold some land, and her mother gave piano lessons and did odd jobs to earn some extra money. Even this was not enough, and when Rachel left, she owed the college quite a large sum of money. She quickly found work to pay her debt off.

At college, Rachel found it difficult to make friends at first. Other students thought she seemed distant. She often went home on weekends, or her mother would come to stay with her at college. Some students made fun of Rachel because of this. After a while, Rachel did make friends by helping people with their work.

Carson was certainly a good student. She graduated with distinction in 1929. She was one of only three students that year to achieve the honor. She also won a summer scholarship to Woods Hole Marine Biological Laboratory in Massachusetts, which was a great honor and opportunity.

Finishing Education

When her summer scholarship was over, Carson went to Johns Hopkins University in Baltimore, Maryland, to study **zoology**. Money was still a problem. After her first year, she had to abandon full-time studying. Carson took a part-time job as an assistant in Raymond Pearl's Biological Research laboratory. There, she worked with rats and fruit flies, which earned her some money to pay for her tuition. During one summer she helped teach zoology at the university's summer school. The following summer, she taught at the Dental and Pharmacy School in Maryland.

Science Notes

Why Study Fruit Flies?

Fruit flies are what is known in biology as a **model organism**. A model organism is a species that is easy to keep and breed in a laboratory and has some particular reason it should be studied. A fruit fly's life span is short, so scientists can observe its entire lifespan in just a few weeks, and generations of flies in a few months. Also, surprisingly, fruit flies share 75 percent of the **genes** that cause disease in humans. Genes control or influence traits inherited from our parents. Studying fruit flies can help cure inherited diseases in humans.

Thomas Hunt Morgan

Thomas Hunt Morgan was an American zoologist who won a Nobel Prize in 1933. He, too, had studied zoology at Johns Hopkins University, around 40 years before Carson was there. Morgan is known for studying the fruit fly in his famous "Fly Room" at Columbia University. His research found that genes are connected in a series on **chromosomes**, which carry inherited traits. His discovery formed the basis of the modern science of **genetics**.

Finally, in 1932, Carson completed her master's degree in marine biology. Sadly, she had to give up plans to study some more. Her father died suddenly, and Rachel needed to care for her aging mother. To support her family, she took a temporary job with the US Bureau of Fisheries, writing educational radio shows. It was a great job for Carson, using both her skill at writing and her knowledge of zoology. She also wrote articles about marine life around the Chesapeake Bay for local newspapers and magazines.

Carson's boss was pleased with her radio series. He asked her to take the civil service exam, so she could work for them full-time. She was at the top of all the applicants, and became only the second full-time professional woman hired by the bureau. Carson was now a junior **aquatic** biologist.

Getting Published

In January 1937, Carson's sister Marian died. She left behind two daughters, Marjorie and Virginia, aged 11 and 12. Carson took the girls in. She was now the only breadwinner for her mother and two nieces. It was a big responsibility. Rachel's elderly mother agreed to look after the girls while Rachel worked to pay the bills.

In fall 1937, *Atlantic Monthly* magazine published an essay that Rachel had originally written for her first fisheries bureau brochure. The article, *Undersea*, was a story about a journey along the ocean floor. Publishers Simon & Schuster liked the article, and contacted Carson. They suggested that she turn it into a book.

After several years of writing, *Under the Sea Wind* was published. The book got excellent **reviews** but didn't sell all that many copies. In the meantime, Carson wrote more and more articles for magazines. Rachel wanted to leave the Bureau of Fisheries, but there were no other suitable jobs around. Her career was going well, however. She was promoted to supervisor, and then became chief editor of publications.

"If there is poetry in my book about the sea, it is not because I deliberately put it there, but because no one could write truthfully about the sea and leave out the poetry."

RACHEL CARSON

By this time, Carson was working on her second book, *The Sea Around Us*. The book is a beautifully written history of the seas and oceans. It was published by Oxford University Press. It was on the *New York Times* bestseller list for 86 weeks and won several awards. After the book's success, Carson left her job and started writing full-time.

Science Notes

How Do People Pollute the Seas?

In *The Sea Around Us*, Carson explains that everything we do on land affects our seas. Some pollution is obvious, such as piping sewage straight into our seas. Other pollution may happen as a result of the Earth's water cycle. Water **evaporates** from the surface of the Earth, rises into the atmosphere, cools and **condenses** into rain or snow clouds, and falls again as rain, snow, sleet, and hail. This water collects in rivers and lakes, soil, and inside some rock, and flows back into the oceans, where the cycle starts again. Pollution in our atmosphere affects our oceans in this way.

Carson was now an established, successful author. Her first book, *Under the Sea Wind*, now appeared on the best-seller list, too. A documentary based on *The Sea Around Us* won the 1953 Academy Award for Best Documentary Feature. However, Carson was not pleased with the documentary, and it was the last time she let anyone film any of her works.

Carson now had some money and was writing full-time. She had a cottage built on Southport Island, Maine. She and her mother spent their summers there by the sea. Rachel became close friends with her neighbor, Dorothy Freeman. The two women both loved nature, and regularly wrote letters to each other when they were apart.

Southport Island

In 1955, Carson finished the third book of her sea series, *The Edge of the Sea*. The book explores the animal and plant life of the rocky coast of New England, the sandy beaches of the mid-Atlantic, and coral shores along the Southern U.S. coast. The book was illustrated by her friend, artist Bob Hines.

Bob Hines had worked for Rachel as an artist at the US Fish and Wildlife Service. Carson and Hines traveled together from Maine to the Florida Keys studying, collecting, and drawing the sea life. Carson insisted each animal they studied was respected, and returned to exactly the same place it came from.

Bob Hines and Rachel Carson explore sea life along the Atlantic coast.

Another Family Tragedy

In 1957, one of Carson's nieces, Marjorie, died. Carson adopted Marjorie's five-year-old son, Roger, and cared for him along with her aging mother. She built a new winter home in Silver Spring, Maryland, to bring up the boy, but they spent their summers in Maine by the sea.

Silent Spring

Carson was becoming increasingly worried about the effect man-made chemicals were having on the environment. The development of **atomic weapons** and new chemicals were all of concern. In a letter to Dorothy Freeman, she wrote:

"I suppose my thinking began to be affected soon after atomic science was firmly established ... It was pleasant to believe that much of Nature was forever beyond the tampering reach of man ... I have now opened my eyes and my mind. I may not like what I see, but it does no good to ignore it."

RACHEL CARSON

In 1962, Rachel Carson's best-known book, *Silent Spring*, was published. The book begins by describing a typical American town. But in this town, sheep and cattle become ill and die. People fall ill with diseases doctors have never seen before. The birds, bees, and fish disappear. There is no fruit on the trees, and no crops grow.

What was the cause? People have poisoned their environment with chemicals. Each effect Carson describes has happened somewhere. Luckily, up to now, no single town has suffered all these effects together, but Carson feared that one day a place might.

Carson was worried that a new **pesticide**, called **DDT**, had been rushed into use before enough research had *been* done on its effect on wildlife. DDT was killing more creatures than just their intended targets, and was being sprayed over huge areas of land.

What Is DDT?

In 1939, Swiss chemist Paul Müller discovered that DDT killed insects. In small amounts, the chemical seemed to be harmless to other wildlife. In 1943, the U.S. Army sprayed over a million people with DDT in Naples, Italy, to stop the spread of a disease known as typhus. It was also used in North America and Europe to stop the spread of malaria by killing the mosquitoes which carried the disease. Müller was awarded the 1948 **Nobel Prize** in Physiology or Medicine for his discovery. By 1959, 40,000 tons of DDT were being sprayed every year on land in the U.S.!

An aircraft spraying DDT over a forest in 1955 to control budworm.

A New Science

Even before *Silent Spring* was published, Carson knew it would cause a stir. *The New Yorker* magazine published pages from the book a few months before it came out. As a result, one pesticide company wrote to the publishers to try to stop the book. Carson and the publishers were not put off. She wanted the public to know the facts about pesticides. As she had said in her letter to Dorothy Freeman, "it does no good to ignore it."

However, Carson did not realize just how influential her book would be. *Silent Spring* is said to be one of the main inspirations behind the science of **ecology**.

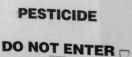

DANGER   PELIGRO

PESTICIDE

DO NOT ENTER

PESTICIDA (VENENO)

NO ENTRE

What Is Ecology?

Ecology is a new science. It is a branch of biology that began during the second half of the 20th century. Ecology studies the relationship of living things to each other, and to what is around them. From the largest animals to the tiniest, microscopic bacteria, the survival of any organism depends on how it copes in its surroundings. The word comes from the Greek, meaning "the study of the house," or the study of the place we live in.

Carson's enemies tried to discredit her. The chemical companies wanted people to keep buying their pesticides. She was labeled a hysterical woman and a poor scientist. Carson was prepared for criticism. She had made sure her claims had been checked by many scientists and other experts, so she knew they were correct.

In response, one chemical company wrote an article, *The Desolate Year,* making fun of *Silent Spring.* It described how terrible the world would be if pesticides didn't exist. The article was sent to newspapers, along with a five-page fact sheet.

Struggling with Illness

Back in 1950, Carson had a lump removed from her breast. After her surgery, doctors thought that she wouldn't need any more treatment. In 1960, while Carson was writing *Silent Spring*, she again developed a lump and had to have surgery. At around the same time, she also suffered from **arthritis** and a problem with her eyes that was so bad there were times when she could not see to read or write.

A TV Appearance

In April, 1963, Rachel Carson appeared on "CBS Reports," an hour-long television news program. People who watched her interview may not have read her book. This TV appearance brought the issue of pesticides into millions of ordinary people's homes. Her clear arguments impressed viewers. Rachel was very ill by the time this documentary was recorded. She was so weak that at some points she needed to prop her head on her hands. The program makers were worried that she would not survive long enough to see the show broadcast.

In America in the 1960s, most households owned a television. There were only three channels; ABC, CBS, and NBC. Families would often watch programs together.

Carson was a private person, and kept quiet about her illness. In a letter to her friend Marjorie Spock, she wrote that she did not want to read about her ailments in the gossip columns, as it would bring too much comfort to the chemical companies!

Also, the chemical companies and the pesticide industry had spent over a quarter of a million dollars trying to persuade the public that Rachel Carson was incorrect. If they knew she had cancer, they might have used that fact against her. It would have been easy to suggest she had made her findings up, and that her book was just written by a dying woman wanting someone to blame for her illness.

Science Notes

Science Advisors

Science can be complex. The average person can't understand every branch of science in depth. Even scientists will usually only be an expert in their own field. Because of this, scientists are often asked to help advise decision makers. After *Silent Spring* was published, President John F. Kennedy asked experts on his Science Advisory Committee to investigate Rachel Carson's claims. Their report agreed with *Silent Spring's* findings.

U.S. President
John F. Kennedy

Before the Senate

I n early June, 1963, despite her illness, Rachel Carson spoke in front of a committee headed by Senator Ribicoff. Ribicoff had seen her TV appearance, and ordered an investigation into pesticide use the very next day. Carson presented a strong case against the use of chemicals. She didn't want to ban all pesticides. Carson instead recommended regulating their use, and banning the most **toxic** ones.

Science Notes

What Does "Toxic" Mean?

If a substance is toxic, it is capable of causing injury or death. A toxic substance might cause cancer, or be poisonous, or harmful to life. Practically every substance is toxic to some degree. Even water can lead to water intoxication if we drink too much of it. How poisonous a substance is, is called its "toxicity." Something with high toxicity would be harmful after just a short exposure to it. Something with low toxicity would take much longer to be harmful. Scientists test substances for their toxicity, and then classify and label them.

One thing that Carson argued strongly against was aerial spraying. Spraying crops from an aircraft meant that pesticides could either accidentally or deliberately be sprayed over people's property without their permission. She described a story of some dairy farmers whose milk had been banned from sale after their land was sprayed against moths without their permission.

Carson believed that a modern-day Bill of Rights would include a right for people to be safe from lethal poisons being used on their private property. Carson argued that the only reason protection against pesticides was not included in the original Bill of Rights was because "our forefathers, despite their considerable wisdom and foresight, could conceive of no such problem."

The Bill of Rights

The Bill of Rights is the first 10 amendments to the United States Constitution. They put limits on what the government could do and control. They protected a person's freedom of religion or freedom of speech, for example.

Carson's Legacy

Rachel Carson died of a heart attack on April 14, 1964, aged 56, at her home in Silver Spring, Maryland. Most of her ashes were buried beside her mother's grave. Her friend Dorothy Freeman scattered the rest along the shore of Southport Island, at one of their favorite spots by the ocean.

Carson left a lasting legacy behind her. Her work helped focus the public's attention on caring for the environment. The lessons learned from reading *Silent Spring* led to a nationwide ban on DDT and other pesticides. The book also inspired an environmental movement that eventually led to the creation of the U.S. Environmental Protection Agency.

When Senator Ribicoff learned of Rachel Carson's death, he spoke for many Americans in telling reporters, "Today we mourn a great lady. All mankind is in her debt."

Some years after her death, in 1980, Carson was awarded the Presidential Medal of Freedom by President Jimmy Carter. The award is, along with the Congressional Gold Medal, the highest civilian award of the United States.

This life-sized statue of Rachel Carson by David Lewis is outside the Marine Biological Laboratory at Woods Hole, Massachusetts.

A Suitable Honor

A number of conservation areas have been named after Carson. In 1969, the Coastal Maine National Wildlife Refuge was named the Rachel Carson National Wildlife Refuge.

Rachel Carson will be remembered for having a beautiful writing style and being a talented, thorough scientist. By bringing these two skills together, she managed to make environmental issues public knowledge through her well-written, best-selling books.

Science Project

Examine the Effect of an Ocean Oil Spill

There are many things that pollute our seas. Large amounts of oil sometimes spill from transport ships that sink in the ocean. What effect do you think that would have on sea life? And why might an oil spill cause seabirds to drown?

Try these experiments to find out how oil pollution affects our seas and oceans.

You Will Need:

- a small container with a lid
- cooking oil
- a handful of sand or gravel
- two bird feathers
- a cup of clean water
- dish soap

1

Fill a container two-thirds full of water and add a handful of sand. This is your ocean. Pour some oil onto the water until it forms a layer. What do you think would happen to animals that need to come to the surface to breathe?

2

Put on the lid and shake the container as if there were a storm in the ocean. Has some of the oil moved to other parts of the ocean? How would the oil affect life at the bottom of the ocean?

3

Feathers have a little natural oil to keep birds from getting waterlogged and sinking. Drop one feather in the cup of clean water and the other in your oily ocean. Do they both float? Clean your oily feather with dish soap and let them both dry.

4

Once they are dry, drop both feathers in clean water. Do they both float as well as each other? The cleaned feather will probably have lost its waterproof coating. What might this mean for a seabird?

Test Your Knowledge

Test your science knowledge and your memory with this quiz about Rachel Carson and her work. Can you get them all right? Answers are at the bottom of page 29.

1 What do marine biologists do?
a) study boats b) sell seaweed c) study sea creatures

2 What type of books did Rachel like to read when she was a child?
a) books about animals
b) adventure stories
c) fantasy stories

3 What was Rachel Carson's most famous book called?
a) *Quiet Summer* b) *Silent Spring* c) *Falling Silent*

4 What is pollution?
a) a substance introduced into the environment that has a harmful or poisonous effect
b) a type of fish
c) a big wave in the ocean

5 What is DDT?

a) a fly b) a bird food c) a chemical used to kill insects

6 What important type of fly did Rachel Carson help to study when she was a student?

a) the housefly b) the firefly c) the fruit fly

7 Which of these is an example of the water cycle?

a) when water evaporates from oceans and then returns to the land as rain.

b) when rock is worn away into sand

c) when a fish eats another fish

8 What way of spraying pesticides did Rachel Carson particularly dislike?

a) spraying from a can

b) spraying from aircraft

c) spraying by a tractor

9 Even water can be toxic if we have too much.

a) true b) false

Answers

1. c – study sea creatures; 2. a – books about animals; 3. b – *Silent Spring*;
4. a – a substance introduced into the environment that has a harmful or
poisonous effect; 5. c – a chemical used to kill insects; 6. c – the fruit fly; 7. a –
when water evaporates from oceans and then returns to the land as rain; 8. b –
spraying from aircraft; 9. a – true

29

Glossary

aquatic   Performed in or on water.

arthritis   Painful, inflamed joints.

atomic weapons   Explosive devices that derive their destructive force from nuclear reactions.

biology   A branch of knowledge that deals with living organisms and life processes.

chromosomes   The bodies of a cell nucleus that contain all or most of the genes.

condenses   Changes from a less dense to a denser form, such as steam condensing to water.

DDT   A colorless insecticide poisonous to many animals.

ecology   A branch of science concerned with the relationships between living things and their environment.

environmental   Relating to the natural world and the impact of human activity on its condition.

evaporates   Passes off into vapor from a liquid state.

genes   Units of heredity transferred from a parent that determine characteristics of the offspring.

genetics   The study of inherited characteristics.

habitats   The place or type of place where a plant or animal naturally lives or grows.

marine biologist   A person that studies or works with a saltwater organism or organisms.

model organism   A species studied because it is easy to keep and breed in a laboratory setting.

Nobel Prize   An annual prize established by the will of Alfred Nobel awarded to people who work for the interests of humanity.

pesticide   A substance used to destroy pests.

pollution   Spoiled with waste made by humans.

reviews   Discussions by a critic about the quality of something.

scholarship   Money given to a student to help pay for further education.

toxic   Poisonous.

zoology   A branch of biology concerned with the animal kingdom and animal life.

For More Information

Fabiny, Sarah. *Who Was Rachel Carson?* New York, NY: Penguin Workshop, 2014.

Hustad, Douglas. *Environmentalist Rachel Carson (STEM Trailblazer Bios).* Minneapolis, MN: Lerner Publications, 2016.

Lawlor, Laurie, and Laura Beingessner. *Rachel Carson and Her Book That Changed the World.* New York, NY: Holiday House Publishers, 2014.

Rowell, Rebecca. *Rachel Carson Sparks the Environmental Movement (Great Moments in Science).* Minneapolis, MN: Core Library, 2016.

Websites
Due to the changing nature of Internet links, PowerKids Press has developed an online list of websites related to the subject of this book. This site is updated regularly. Please use this link to access the list:

www.powerkidslinks.com/wcs/carson

Index